ISOMETRIC LORE

MCF

QUOTATIONS 2004 - 2008

Isometric Lore

Copyright © 2008 by Mel C. Finley
All rights reserved under International and
Pan-American laws.

Published by:

ISOMETRIC LORE
P.O. Box 808
Seal Beach, CA 90740
www.mcfstudioz.com

Available online at: www.lulu.com

ISBN# 978-0-615-25032-8

ACKNOWLEDGMENTS

Cover Design & Consulting
Gary Takesian

Front Cover Art: GOD CLOWNS
Artist: Mel Finley aka MCF
Photographer: Chris Lee

Back Cover Photography:
Frances Clare

SPECIAL THANKS & BLESSINGS TO

Maynard & Opal, Foundation

Richard Madeira, Angel

Dean Hart, F. it

Dennis Wilson, The Master going Faster

Julie Baxley, Healing Hands

I Ling Sun, Healing Long Needles

Mic Ja, Grace of Soul

Agape International Spiritual Center

Santa Fe, New Mexico, Sunset

American Express, Blue

The Herb Superb, No Comment

Sauvignon Blanc

La Salina, B.C. Cottage by the Sea

The Archangels I'm not aware of.

The Creator, I call GOD.

BY the way,

I only wrote down the following words.

This GOD and I have reached an agreement.

I don't claim to be the source of the material

and this GOD will from time to time

allow me to take the word out for a spin.

Meditation: There is no one moment of quieted silence that exists behind closed eyes that does not exist in front of them, Eyes wide open.

It's the work of a philosopher to define the unknown by describing its affect on what is known.

It's a three-pound brain against a gazillion tons of protoplasm,... what'd you expect?

I see God as a non-perishable item.
I see myself as a savvy consumer.

Your status in Oneness can be enhanced
but never advanced.

The soul has a shelf life.

GOD would be the ideal companion if it were not for its overwhelming superiority and…it's such a control freak.

I'm a student of God.
Anyone closer to God, raise your
hand………Thank You…didn't think so.

Cleanliness is next to resale value.

Religions will learn to live with one
another in harmony _not_ when they agree
on one book to read but when each and
every one of their followers
writes their own.

I eat meat, but it's from animals that died from natural causes.

I'm one of the greatest indoors-men of my time.

You use violence because you don't know how to use love.

Loneliness is a mansion
companionship is a capsule.

**One's own heart should be in order
before franchising it.**

**Mantra: Sacred Syllables.
How many syllables in GOD?**

Guilt is the original inside trader.

Computers will be smarter than humans, just as soon as we humans figure out how to do it.

There is no Hell, however
there are two lines to get into Heaven.
One requires no effort on your part
The other requires a lifetime of
compassion & sacrifice.
The latter is the short one.

**Physical limitations are God's Idea,
as are spiritual dimensions...
They are definitely not mine.**

**The body always wants to die.
How much do you want to surrender
each hour?**

**All of existence is the conscious
uncontrollable drift toward the Creator's
resolve/dissolve.**

When you comprehend that your soul's
sojourn has no end or beginning you
achieve your soul's goal...act accordingly.

When you describe with certainty Sin,
you forfeit your right to participate in Salvation,
yours specifically.

Stressed out doesn't come from being
overwhelmed by events,
it comes from not being grateful for the
one moment now at hand.

**Who is smarter men or women?
It's whichever one
<u>isn't</u> asking the question.**

*To my feet it is a journey.
To my soul it's rest,
what is to awaken never slept.*

God's Math: Every action has an equal and opposite, cross to bear.

All of religion is a third party in a two-way conversation with God.

Same word new generation open to a loose interpretation.

**There's your road to Zen and then there is the Creator's.
...Care to guess who prevails?
Yours has you exalted or accomplished.
The Creator's has you spent & the same.**

Before there was evil there was memory, remember?

**I have opted to become an inward spectator.
I've discovered my darkest secrets there and they're yours.**

The greatest temptation/sin is the urge to improve your oneness.

**Worrying & lying are of a waste of imagination...
while contemplation & creativity are essential to truth.**

I fear not that I will not be widely known but that I'll be widely known and wildly misunderstood.

**Nobody's from Mars or Venus.
We are all from the planet Nurturing.
Each and every one of us is built
differently from the same clay.
We all bring baggage/damage/not
enough love into a relationship.
But when it comes to becoming a union,
nurturing is what binds us.
It's the only thing that will sustain
everlasting love.**

*When you get to the pearly gates, St. Peter
will ask you one question and it's not how
many sins did you accumulate or not.
It's "How did you serve GOD?"*

Women will realize true equality when each and every one of them designs their own clothing line.

I'm in love with IS.

Spiritual Evolution:

1000 Gods.
1 God but a thousand prophets.
1 God too many prophets and 10,000 religions.
1 God, no prophets no religions, billions of disciples.
1 Love.

Leave this world expectedly.

*A successful relationship is one
whose components
nurture each other's selflessness.
It's successful because each implodes into a
oneness that is neither, yet echoes in both
evermore. Alas, a love death could not part.*

It's the summer of the heart's April.
An ambrosia wind is working a horizon of
orange deaf stillness.
Day and light are of equal enlightenment.
Azure mist Sanskrit mountains warmed
from perpetual flames unseen.
Spiritual clouds impersonating
hookah smoke,
pools of falling breathing schooled water,
witnessed by elder greenwoods.
Deer eyed wee creatures dinning out.
Space to know timeless listening.

This God's universe is an ocean of waves
we call moments or now. There are those
who focus and float on the waves.
Others contemplate and commune with
the ocean's magnitudes.
We all swim, when you swim know this
one truth.
Every stroke is of equal value in this
God's math and as such,
perfect for any swim. Love your swim,
this ocean is one giant lifeguard.

It's the self that asks of the self,
total selflessness.
It's the self that must sadly inform the
self of its irresponsibility.

**The Art of conversation
was never an art form.
Nor was your opinion.
Art has a longer shelf life than opinions.**

**There are 3 stages of spiritual evolution.
They progress as follows:
One is known by a state of unconsciousness.
One is a state of mindful and constant consciousness.
One is presence without conscious effort.**

*The vision within is greater than the
distance of time, it requires no insight.*

*The man that works to fulfill himself is a
candidate for a hollow life.
The man who works to fulfill a life
other than his,
is the caretaker of the creator's estate.*

**It's a successful life when compassion is
your default emotion.**

*Move through each day, assuming you're
loved, and admit your loving.*

In a *sometime* anywhere you will know
Knowing All
See sight without light.
Touch sensation without softer.
Hear truth without mention
Be the butterfly
Exist as bliss
Smell passion
Become blessings wherewithal,
…. *An Easy Kiss.*

Healthy Fat

I am by nature fat; grace of God tips the scale.
My girth, circumference, gets my arms around everything.
Size matters, big in life is small of selfish.
You make sun that weights when you're of less shadow.
God's cheeseburger, animal style,
is nurturing.
Nurturing is never fast food,
however nurturing is quick to do,
embrace longer.
There is only one calorie, God,
Gorge on **fatso.**

The truth of who you are is meaningless
without the test of God's map-less,
hedge-less labyrinth.
Good news: You're always centered,
spiral spiritual continuum.
There can be no road less traveled
occupying God's area.
Stray? Yah, Really? ... Good Fking Luck...
No Can Do, Your oneness.
"I am that you should know
the end all be all is IS."
"You're chasing your tail."

It's not that the mind-body-spirit wants
to disobey some higher power.
It wants to be less at the mercy of
circumstance.
Yes the maker provides the wind and
man raises said sail.
Man captains a sailboat solely dependent
on the whim of the maker's breath and at
the zenith of its gust of wisdom must
scuttle it.

There is a light that shines bright in darkness.
It emanates from both ends of the tunnel.

The world will live as one when it gives
up the concept of one world.

Beginninglessness, as you Were, Why?

*We're so much alike
we who are of one.
That if I were to tell you I love you,
It would be a form of narcissism.*

If You Tithe as part of a rewards
program... You don't get it.
If you Tithe out of some sense of
obligation,.. You don't get it.
If you Tithe to overwhelm another with
blessings paid-forward,..
They get it you got it.

It matters not that you're free from your
thoughts of fruition.
It does matter that the mind is adrift in
nirvana.

The simplest way to change
the thinking of another
is to listen without expression,
then split.

Our/Your soul is in harmony with the
universe at all times,
in multiplicity and in dualities, during the
influx of spiritual graces
and torrents of timeless test, and yes
even when you're f**d-up.

Your relationship with God is always
personal and intimate.
Your religion and spiritual practices
are redundant.

Poverty must be an aphrodisiac.

Whatever experience that has been
suggested of life beyond death
is and can only be fictional. Reincarnation?,
a do over?,
not in God's anti-superfluous math.
Spirit merely defines our space in
the great soul.
Only the fear of that spirit extinguished
would come up with something as
2 dimensional as
an ascending or descending soul or one that
is farmable.

The human body is a robe for the spirit to put on
in order to answer the door of oneness.
The robe is perishable as is the spirit,
however the robe's demise is from deterioration
the spirit's is from acceleration.

Men Have tits too.

The second coming… Evidently somebody can't count.

It's a funny thing about compassion,
when you use IT,
IT always works.

I'm alone because I didn't leave much for people to care for and nothing extraordinary for them to care about.

Move through God not to God.

Was there doing that, here now doing that.

One thing we all have in common is
we truly don't know what happens
after we die.
Another is our desperate need to speculate.

I DON'T KNOW.
The 3 words the upright &
clever/knowing/enlightened Fear.
So they invent, pontificate and war.

What energy is negative if all energy is
necessary and of value?

If you've lived your life to gain the world's affection and approval you've lived your life for two people, yourself and whoever was too busy gaining the attention of the world to love you.

Alcohol is the preferred coping mechanism for the damaged and daredevils. The rest of us prefer infatuation, meditation and a really good cheeseburger.

Good luck teaches us nothing while misfortune is the cornerstone of wisdom.

Don't marry a moving target.

The Bible is a short story; Love and Forgive, the rest is Sin.

I have a reoccurring dream; in it I'm in a constant state of awakening.

#1 Fight #2 Flee #3 Group n Discuss #4 Be Still.

Spiritual prosperity flows through us not to us.
S0...What is it you wish to keep?

Mistakes are the seeds of wisdom.
Farm them with plenty of sunshine.

I choose to speak to the living we do,
not the living we imagine
we'll do afterlife.

I'm not from here, never was but for
now.
Time travels to me, around me, through
me.
Mine is a stopwatch running never
stopping,
an hourglass of which the sand runs
eternally.

Luck: The vicar of math, the sacker of Logic.

Cherish is the 1st vow to go.

All of existence is something to get tired of with one exception, existence. IS.

I have serious concerns about a generation that cannot figure out how to wear a baseball hat.

Is bliss being in tune with now or detached from the temporary of each & every one of them? Simultaneously both? .... What?

Credit is worth assumed.
Finance charges are worth realized.

The trick of the devil is to have you believe you obtain,
that you move from 2nd to 1st. In GOD, where allthingsareone, you always and only move from 1st to 1st.
So Then, why are we here?
Perhaps to learn that 1st to 1st does more for your self-esteem
than 2nd to1st.
OR
You can do that which you have not done but you will not be more than you have been and are.

God's math adds to and subtracts from our living as cadet archangels. In our time someone will take white chalk to a blackboard and in a calculus graffiti explain every thought.
Blue chalk to a green board, they'll provide the physics recipe for the creation of a soul.
The equations born in the originator cell germinate eternity.
The arithmetic by design demands that all of creation be nurtured. Why? I'm guessing because God's nurturing nature is without formula.
At God's core something without math emanates pure nurturing.
It lives and breathes in density in every cell in our known universe.
However, it habitually resides and is most at home in
the compassionate heart.

We are drawn to and long for a state of being whose capacity is one faculty removed from God's unremitting desire to see us dissolved into endlessness.

We come from God we go to God. Remember the cross-town traffic, learn to love it; it's your saving grace.

Love mainly, trust few, learn to paddle your own canoe.

Nothing is as critical as everything is important.

**Patience will ward off the half hearted
but will only infuriate the determined.**

Violence is the body's immune system externalized.
Violence is a natural occurrence in this God's
chemistry of math.
In a math where all equations equal one,
evidently violence has value.
Humans however choose to primarily concern
themselves with the violent actions and reactions of
those living organisms with eyes.
If humans achieve a spiritual championship and
one fine now harness the power of God and
manipulate a state of pure consciousness,
they will in that physics-less summer
finally realize a season of non-violence.

*To every meaningful purpose
there is no particular time.
Evolution isn't a motion
it's a ramification of illusion.*

**Chase fame and you apprehend 2 things,
attention & unwanted attention.**

**Behave as spiritual immigrants; any
territory you homestead is leased.**

Know no place to place yourself from faith's fate.

Prayer is asking God to change.

**All things in God agree at one point,
but never at once.**

**When life after death is the bedrock of your faith,
life is not as God intended.
God-zillions of time were spent to make
Is, you... BE!**

**Every thought has but two journeys.
One leads to passing pleasure and the
other to perennial bliss.
God embraces both.**

**Life is better for you when you live your life
to serve someone other than yourself.
We revere most those who sacrifice for
another's well being.
That sacrifice requires no degree, title or
spiritual enlightenment.**

**The list of self-pleasuring deeds is as
long as the road to nirvana.**

I wondered in a time when questions
mattered as much as answers.

Wisdom is a child's sport.

The 2nd born is always a Democrat.

The Waters of Lethe, voluntary amnesia.
When you avoid the past you forfeit the
opportunity to forgive it.
There is no future more vengeful than
the past un-forgiven.

*The self-involved self implodes,
forms a black hole.
That vacuum expands until you explode
and shower matter with selfless-service.*

A guru has only one enlightened answer,
Silence accompanied by grinning eyes.

*Life Is Fair.
It's your scoreboard that's wacky.*

The world of matter is to nurture.
The world of spirit is to adore.
When these two worlds are treated as
one God is a success.

**The mind is always moving in a direction
of greater interest, greater satisfaction,
more happiness, more bliss, less conflict,
less pain and eventually
less of the need for being.**

**Given that all things are One,
what is reincarnation?**

**Miracles & Chance.
In a universe of orchestrated math
that knows no chaos?**

Karma: If we indeed return to live again as refried moments because we have not learned now to live correctly, who among us is it safe to take advice from?

**Just because you can't get your arms around it
doesn't mean it doesn't deserve an embrace.**

*Vast vistas, liberating omnipresence,
unconscious richness.
Across forty orders of magnitudes
and one ego border.
The world is here for you,
not to meditate or vegetate away
but use to mass-produce compassion for the
10,000 things.*

Faith: Trusting something you don't completely trust.

The door forward is closed, barred by the self,
to pass the answer given cannot be personal.
Shadows shadow me; time will in time evaporate
me 'til I'm in a moment that does not require me
to remember. 'Til then I maneuver, veer into the
north gust, the azure storm,
come to an easy presence, no distance
diminished, unbridgeable....
never again as anything individual.

Nature has no pecking order,
It was man's idea to establish a totem pole.

Human beings are born of matter once a sun. In the beginning we were cold blooded. It may well be our end as well.

All spiritual experiences are sensations in the body. Nothing could be more material than the sensation of nirvana.

The Secret: You don't have to obtain or be successful at anything to be happy and completely fulfilled.

The less you desire of life
the fewer are your sufferings.
Refrain from all wants other than
compassion, nurturing and service.
Suffering for these will never require a
coping mechanism.

Sit in silence and you will not hear God.
Be still and you will not feel God.
Move as chaotic as the clouds
that thunder, look to own no one thing
and you will understand God.

A Life fulfilled is not the result of a complete
withdrawal from your senses;
Quite the opposite.
Not one thing in creation
is given a center forever.
The clock on the wall, the sun rising,
do not tell time or age.
Everything in space and time
leaves a footprint.
Wear your best sandals.

**Enlightenment is just one more thing
you'll have to detach from if you wish to
be one with God.**

*All things are an illusion.
And not one of them is without real consequence.*

**Predictable automation and or a
discipline all too familiar
are not the ways of the soul.
The wherewithal to embrace perpetual
new and nurture it without hesitation
is the one & only purpose for breath.**

**Are you spiritually evolving?
What spiritual evolution takes place without
your conscious effort? The greater question
is; is it possible not to spiritually evolve?**

Withdraw to a within and stillness with no
thought, you will then catch your breath.
Come forth to an expressiveness of actions of
compassion in mindful service, to catch God's
breath. God only exhales. Inhale.

Greater consciousness is in the end
still just your opinion.

The 10 step program that is the ladder to nirvana
is the invention of the four chambered muscle
and it's cohort, the two sided CPU AKA: noggin.
The single centrifugal force that steadies it is
the CPU's opinion of the Maker's intentions.
Your CPU's chasing your CPU's tail.

What is to be after death is not to be known,
we have only our suspicions and a clue,....
All things participating in time vanish.

We can never be simply in the now as long as the mind is occupied by the idle hopes of what will/should be now.

Nature vs. Nurturing
Nurture one single desire and it will become your nature.

*We're all soul mates,
but you have to start somewhere.*

The brain does not cause thought
without your permission.

God created evolution, chaos & atheism.
Next question.

*Religion; is a good drink
till you mix it with territory.*

**We are born finished.
We spend our lives comprehending it.**

*You manifest your own state of being, your
own heaven, your own external world,
its adverse notions and blessings.
You do not manifest your oneness.
Consciousness has one soul...
yours is a transient host.*

**The central command for all of
consciousness has no center.**

The path of spiritual evolution returns
consciousness to its source
not as existence but as presence.

**We are born of an origin beyond what
science and technology can
at this time fathom. If some choose to call it
GOD, why would I disagree? Hey it's a start,
we're beginners chasing our tails.**

**Your soul is illuminated and enlightened
not by the events of the heart or
accomplishments of the mind
but by the persistence of time/space and
IS.**

The lethargy present in eternity.
The neuropsychological phenomena that is
nirvana. The soul waiting for resolve then
dissolve. However you define the existence
of a God...or not, subatomic, quantum
random or bang without cause.
One fact cannot be questioned.
All of existence is intentional.

There are 4 truths:
Your truth. My truth. The truth.
The truth about truth.

We wish to find companionship that sees
us for who we really are.
We ask our companion to be there for our
inevitable changes.
We accomplish this with a series of
disposable masks.

The secret is one of two laws.
The law of attraction.
The law of releasing.
One law serves man, the other serves GOD.
One is an affirmation for personal blessings,
One is the only affirmation aligned with GOD.
One claims to be a secret.
One, God makes known with every breath.

I remembered one thing
I learned one thing
I know one thing
They're the same thing.

As long as there is a black vote,
there will be racism.
As long as there is a need for cheap labor,
children will work to eat.
As long as there is political genius,
dictators will be elected.
As long as Love & Compassion continue to
expand the latter are doomed for extinction.

God will prevail and beings will exist in a world of compassion.
As to how long that might take, well this God took a bazillion years to come up with a dinosaur...
I wouldn't hold your breath.

For best results, follow these instructions:

Focus/dwell only on the results you expect.

Wake-up every morning and dismiss yesterday's accomplishments as history, return to square one grateful just to be.

Remember that in the end the aforementioned actions and subsequent results change nothing of your worth in oneness. Don't chase our tail.

*When you live in the now you frequently
forget where you put your glasses.*

**You have but one true enemy,
your subconscious mind.
Who/What kept you from giving?**

**My 1st breath had a time and date,
such will be my last.
Those between that are drawn and exhaled
with deliberate mindfulness to nurture are
the only perfect moments in life.**

*Divorce only the thought that you're alone AND
don't let compassion be the one
that got away.*

What's on your mind is in your life.

The soul has matter and occupies space.
That it would be limited to your physical
dimensions is a stretch.

ART is in the eye of the beholder.
Unless, evidently, you're an appraiser and or
a collector with a ton of cash
and low self esteem.
Never trust the opinion of anyone
with an MFA.
Remember they're operating from a point of
view that's submerged in a tank
of already been done.
While your work is swimming in an ocean of
primordial whim. Haven said that remember
that true creativity is the convenient lack
of total recall.

I have 2 people existing within me.
My inner child who is all about
Discipline? Who? What?
And the women who is trapped inside.
Not to worry ladies as it turns out,
fortunately, she's a lesbian.

*What kind of GOD
lets you question GOD ?*

THE LAST INSIGHT

A bead of water is born outside The Lake
to learn of The Lake.
The bead returns to The Lake.
The bead of water again stands outside
The Lake to know the sacred mystery and
wisdom of The Lake.
The bead of water again returns to
The Lake. The bead of water again and
again stands outside The Lake
to embrace via discipline a way to be
<u>with</u> The Lake.
The bead of water repeats the cycle of
outside and return until
the bead seeks to be The Lake and never
again the bead.
Your soul, piece of the greater soul, is for
releasing not retaining.
Return to God
what has always been borrowed.

**NEXT PUBLICATION
WORK IN PROGRESS:**

THE PLIGHT FOR PLIGHTLESSNESS

THIS IS THE LAST PAGE BEFORE THE MANDATORY BLANK PAGE

PEACE IN   WAR OUT

www.ingramcontent.com/pod-product-compliance
Lightning Source LLC
Chambersburg PA
CBHW032011080426
42735CB00007B/574